Dog Training

The Ultimate Dog Training Bundle

Training Basics And How To Effectively Train An Obedient Dog Without Being A Dog Whisperer

By Vivaco Books

© Copyright 2014 – Vivaco Books

ISBN-13: 978-1534630062
ISBN-10: 1534630066

ALL RIGHTS RESERVED. No part of this publication may be reproduced or transmitted in any form whatsoever, electronic, or mechanical, including photocopying, recording, or by any informational storage or retrieval system without express written, dated and signed permission from the author.

Table of Contents

DOG TRAINING BASICS 1

Introduction 3
    What This Book Is About 3

Chapter 1: What Everyone Ought To Know About Dog Training 7
    How Dogs Learn 8

Chapter 2: How To Choose The Right Training Method 13
    Dog Training Methods 14

Chapter 3: The 4 Most Important Dog Training Concepts 23
    Basic Dog Training Concepts 24

Chapter 4: The 5 Standard Commands Every Dog Should Know 29
    Basic Obedience Commands For Dogs 30

Chapter 5: House Manners For Dogs 37
    House Essentials For Dogs 38

Chapter 6: F.A.Q. - Frequently Asked Questions 43

What is dog training? 43
How can I choose the right training? 44
What is the difference between corrections and rewards? 45
Why should I train my dog? 45
Is it true that some dog breeds are "un-trainable?" 46
When is the right time to begin dog training? 46
Which behavioral problems can dog training programs solve? 47
Who is the boss when training the dog? 47
Does positive reinforcement training means allowing your dog to do whatever he wants to? 48

Conclusion 49
DOG OBEDIENCE TRAINING 53
Introduction 55
Chapter 1: Dog Obedience Training 101: You Ought To Know This Before Training Your Dog 57
Benefits Of Obedience Training (To Your Dog) .. 58
Benefits Of Dog Training (To You) 62

Chapter 2: Obedience Training Devices - The Ones You Truly Need 67
Collars 69

Leash 73

Clicker 73

Head Halter.. 74

Chapter 3: 6 Mistakes Beginners Usually Make and How to Avoid Them..77

#Mistake No1: Wrong thing right time/ Right thing wrong time 78

#Mistake No2: The gentle but firm giant 79

#Mistake No3: Lest you forget 80

#Mistake No4: Hygiene is not a compromise...... 81

#Mistake No5: Show some love to the crate........ 82

#Mistake No6: Looking at training from a negative side... 83

Chapter 4: Basic Training: How To Properly Teach Your Dog These 5 Essential Commands 85

How to teach your dog the sit command............... 86

How to teach your dog the down command........ 87

How to teach your dog the heel command........... 89

How to teach your dog the come command 90

How to teach your dog the stay command........... 91

Chapter 5: Advanced Training: Three Advanced Commands For Dogs - Are You Ready To Kick It Up

A Notch? 93
    How to teach your dog the "watch me" command
.... 94
    How to teach your dog the "place" command 95
    How to teach your dog the "steady" command ... 96

Conclusion 99

DOG TRAINING BASICS

All In One Startup Guide

By Vivaco Books

Introduction

What This Book Is About

This book contains proven methods and solid information regarding dog training from a beginner's perspective. It was designed with simplicity in mind and as a short guide that will provide you with all the necessary information regarding dog training so as to make better choices.

You are most likely a new dog owner, or maybe you owned a dog before, but never tried to train it properly. In any case, adding a dog into you and your family's life is a big commitment. Training a dog takes time, effort and patience. It may seem difficult at times, but the reward of having a healthy trained furry friend is definitely worth it.

You are going to learn what dog training is and why it is so important. We have summarized the most popular training methods available, so you can find out which one would best suit you and your canine.

You will learn the 4 most important basic training concepts, which you can apply instantly and see results, regardless of training methods.

You will also find out the 5 standard commands that every dog owner should know and every dog should follow, in order to have a healthy and happy relationship with each other.

Finally, if you intend to keep your dog inside your home, you will learn some house manners that your dog should understand and follow, so that it won't bring down your house.

Thank you for purchasing this book. We hope you enjoy it!

Chapter 1:
What Everyone Ought To Know About Dog Training

Dog training refers to the modification process of a dog behavior, either for the dog to help in particular activities or perform specific tasks, or for the dog to effectively participate in typical domestic life.

While dog training for particular duties goes way back, their training to be compatible pets started in the

1950s. The dog learns from each interaction that it has with the environment. This chapter highlights what dog training focuses on to achieve the training purpose.

How Dogs Learn

Operant/Instrumental conditioning

This form of learning allows a dog's behavior to be modified by the consequences. There are 2 complementary motivations that drive instrumental learning: the minimization of aversive outcomes and the maximization of positive ones.

There are basically two methods of reinforcing or strengthening behavior: Positive Reinforcement is where a behavior becomes strengthened by the production of certain desirable consequences while Negative Reinforcement is where a behavior becomes strengthened by the avoidance of some undesirable consequences.

Typical positive reinforcement situations satisfy certain psychological and physiological needs; hence it can be in the form of food, demonstration of affection or a game. Different dogs find various things reinforcing. Negative reinforcement happens when the dog discovers that a specific response terminates the presentation of any aversive stimulus. Aversive may be anything that a dog doesn't like; for example, a tight choking chain.

Classical conditioning

This is a form of learning where a single stimulus, the conditioned one, signals a second stimulus to occur, the unconditioned stimulus.

Classical conditioning is basically when the dog learns to familiarize itself with things in the environment, or realizes that certain things go together. The dog may be frightened of rain by associating it with lightning and thunder, or the dog may respond to its owner putting on a specific pair of shoes by getting its leash.

This method is employed in dog training to aid it in making particular associations with a specific stimulus, in order to overcome fear of situations or people.

Non-associative learning

This is a response change to stimulus that does not include association of the presented stimulus with an event or even another stimulus like punishment or reward. There are two forms of non-associative learning: habituation and sensitization.

A good example of habituation is when a dog that often reacts excitedly to a door alarm is subjected to repeated ringing until it stops responding to this meaningless stimuli.

The dog will become habituated to such a noise. Some reactions to stimuli may become stronger rather than habituating to repeated event or stimuli. This is where desensitization comes in handy.

Desensitization involves pairing positive reactions with objects, people, or conditions that causes anxiety or fear. Consistent exposure to feared objects or rewards, such as fireworks, reduces the dog's stress, thereby making it desensitized.

Social learning

This is influenced by the behavior of others. It does not require reinforcement to take place, but rather a model. It involves observing, remembering and imitating behaviors. Domestic dogs are social animals and their social dependency enables them to learn the behavior of other dogs.

The term "social learning" covers many closely linked concepts: mimicking or allelomimetic behavior where puppies copy others, social facilitation where another dog causes increased behavior intensity and local enhancement that includes social facilitation pieces, trial-and-error learning and mimicking.

Chapter 2:
How To Choose The Right Training Method

Dog training involves teaching a dog to obey various commands given by the master. There are various dog training methods and each of them has its own share of advantages and disadvantages. People who are looking for the right dog training method for their pet must consider the amount of time they would devote to dog training, their patience, how smart their dog appears to be, as well as the dog's preferences.

The characteristics of any successful method include knowing your dog's personality and attributes, accuracy in timing reinforcement or punishment, as well as consistent communication. Here are the major dog training methods you can choose depending on the above factors.

Dog Training Methods

Koehler Method

The Koehler method is based on the philosophy that dogs often act on their rights to choose their actions. The method emphasizes that every dog's learned behavior/action is a matter of choice which solely depends on their personal learning experience. When these choices are driven by the expectation of some reward, such a behavior will probably be repeated.

On the other hand, when they are driven by anticipation of some sort of punishment, they will likely go away. Once your dog learns that the choices lead to discomfort or comfort, it can then be taught to always make the right decisions.

Action-Memory-Desire is the learning pattern that this method employs; the dog will act, remember the consequences, and then form the willingness to avoid or repeat the consequences.

Adherents of this method often believe that after a behavior has been taught correctly, it should be enacted so that any subsequent correction would be fair, expected and reasonable.

This method has been used for several years, but some of the prescribed punishment procedures are now considered unnecessary, inappropriate and inhumane by several trainers.

Motivational Training

Motivational or positive training uses reward in reinforcing good behavior, while ignoring the bad behavior.

This is based on Thorndike's Law of Effect which states that actions that result in rewards will become more frequent and those that don't result in rewards will become less frequent.

Pure positive dog training is possible, but hard, as it calls for patience and time to regulate the rewards that the dog gets for its behavior.

Clicker training

This is a positive reinforcement dog training system that depends on operant conditioning. It employs conditioned reinforcers that are delivered more rapidly and precisely as compared to primary reinforcers like food.

The key to effective delivery of this dog training method is accurate timing by delivering a particular conditioned reinforcer at the time when a desired behavior is exhibited. The clicker focuses on entrenching a good behavior in a dog by luring it by using reinforcers such as hand gestures or treats. After the dog learns the behavior, the treat and the clicker is stopped.

Clicker training does not employ physical corrections or compulsions. It is majorly based on positive reinforcements.

Certain clicker trainers employ mild corrections like a non-reward marker: "Whoops" or "Uhuh" to make the dog realize that a behavior is not right, or corrections like "Time out" in which attention to the dog is withdrawn.

Electronic training

This entails the use of an aversive tool like an electric shock. Common types include remotely triggered collars or those that can be triggered by barking, fencing which gives a shock when a dog with a special collar goes over a buried wire, and special mats placed on the furniture to give some type of shock. Certain aids produce an aversive like citronella spray when triggered.

Electronic dog training has generated a lot of controversy. Those who support it say that employing electronic device in training dogs permits distance training and can eliminate self-rewarding behavior.

They also claim that if well used, they have a reduced risk of injury and stress compared to mechanical devices, like choke chains.

Opponents point out the serious risks of psychological and physical trauma that can be caused by abusive or incorrect use.

Model-rival training

Based on social learning principles, this type of training employs a model and a rival for attention in demonstrating the desired behavior. This training method was initially used by Irene Pepperberg in training a parrot to label various objects.

After that, Young and McKinley undertook a study whether this method can be used to train domestic dogs. The study generated the required results since the origin and nature of the dog allows observational learning.

Dominance-based training

This is based on the belief that "dogs are wolves" and because wolves have hierarchical packs in which the alpha male rules, humans must therefore dominate dogs so as to modify their behavior.

Animal behaviorists claim that the use of dominance

in modifying the behavior may suppress the dog's behavior without solving the root cause of a problem. It may exacerbate a problem and elevate the dog's aggression, fear, and anxiety.

Dogs subjected to continuous threats might react aggressively. This may happen because the dogs feel afraid and threatened and not because they are trying to acquire dominance.

Relationship-based training

This is derived from symbolic interactionism theories and uses the patterns of adjustment, communication, and interpretation between the trainers and the dogs.

By building a positive relationship, this method intends to achieve results which will benefit the trainer and the dog alike as well as strengthen and enhance their relationship.

The fundamental principles include:

\# Making sure the dog's basic needs are met prior to commencing training.

\# Knowing what motivates the canine and employing that to influence its behaviors.

\# Interpreting the dog's body language for better communication between you and the dog.

\# Using positive reinforcement for desired behavior.

\# Teaching compatible behaviors instead of unwanted behaviors.

\# Controlling its environment to prevent unwanted behaviors.

In conclusion someone should take into consideration many factors prior to choosing the right training method that will be best suited for him as well as his dog.

Chapter 3:
The 4 Most Important Dog Training Concepts

When you bring a dog home, it needs more than just care, love and other basic needs. For a healthy and good dog/ human relationship, dog training is necessary as this enables it to learn the mannerisms needed to survive in society.

Each discipline stems around specific basic principles. Animal behavior and dog training is no different. There are some basic dog training concepts that guide the whole process.

Basic Dog Training Concepts

Manage

Management hinders undesired behaviors from developing into habits by reducing or eliminating opportunities for dogs to rehearse such a behavior and hence develop an environment where a dog is always "correct" by default. It includes things like puppy proofing, leash use, crate training, using no-pull device, etc. It can be used together with rewards for success.

For instance, one can use no-pull devices for the dog to walk well on the leash, and reward him if he manages to walk at your side. Once the dog learns the behavior, fade out the tool and rewards gradually.

Reward

The reward can include anything the dog desires and will work for to earn. The common type is food, but toys, petting, play, and praise are better rewards for some dogs. It can also be an opportunity to do something it enjoys, like going through open doors, playing with other dogs, chasing after a rabbit, or being permitted to sit on the couch.

These real life rewards are often underutilized yet they are very powerful. Integrating these rewards in your routine interactions with the dog, will give you the opportunity to train it frequently without additional effort or extra gear.

Giving the dog rewards without earning them will eventually make the rewards meaningless. A dog wouldn't want to work if it is able to get privileges and rewards for free. Most people grasp this quickly since it applies to meals, but the same logic applies to other rewards.

Allowing the dog to run through the door at will is not safe and also eliminates potentially better opportunities to reward him for good behavior. The dog should sit and watch you as you open the door. Release the dog only after complying with the command.

Ignore

Simply ignore any irritating behavior and the dog will stop it with time. Be selective on the behaviors to ignore. Some of them are self-reinforced and tend to worsen if ignored, like chewing on all items, marking inside the house, or cat chasing. The technique is more effective when your dog is trying to get attention, like jumping on people, begging for a meal, hand nudging, barking for a treat or attention. When demanding attention, even negative attention like scolding can be seen as a reward.

These bad attention-seeking behaviors will diminish faster if you ignore them, although they can become worse temporarily before the dog gives up. Be consistent and ensure the dog ignores any unwanted behavior all the time, or it won't work.

Correct

Offering rewards or ignoring bad behavior won't work if there is something more rewarding in its environment. Harassing wild animals, cats, or livestock, jumping on kids or grabbing clothes or car chasing are examples of self-reinforcing and enjoyable behaviors in dogs that can be very dangerous too. In such cases, correcting or punishing the dog's behavior is appropriate.

Correcting a dog for undesired behavior is a popular concept. It's however important to know that "correcting" doesn't necessarily mean "punishing," it means fixing or making it right.

For instance, one can correct the dog's position by making it stand or sit gently, or tugging the drag line. This isn't really punishing, the dog has simply been shown to do the "correct" thing.

One should consider punishment only after they have performed preliminary work with the use of other methods, beginning with low destruction level up to highly demanding situations. One shouldn't punish their dogs for anything that they haven't taught them adequately.

Manage the highly distracting conditions while you train your dog up through gradually increasing distractions. When a given correction is necessary, one should employ the minimal punishment or correction to get the work done. This will mainly rely on your dog's temperament, training level, and also the distraction level.

When correcting your dog, focus on helping him to make the "right" decisions next time, rather than taking out your frustrations on him or showing him who the boss is.

Chapter 4:
The 5 Standard Commands Every Dog Should Know

Dogs can be great companions, but to enjoy their company more, there are some dog obedience rules that owners must teach their pet dogs. One obvious benefit of teaching your dog obedience is discipline.

When the dog responds to commands such as "stay," "sit," or "come," their management in public or at home, especially with larger breeds, becomes a blessing. Here are the basic obedience commands for every dog.

Basic Obedience Commands For Dogs

Sit

The aim of this command is to make the dog sit on his hindquarters while the front part of the body is placed on the front legs. It can be taught in three different ways.

The first one requires you to watch when the dog is about to sit and if he tries to do so, give the command "sit" in a clear and loud manner. Praise him once the hindquarters reach the ground.

Puppies react to this training technique quite fast. But older dogs may need a dog training treat. Stand in front of your dog and then guide the treat from the dog's nose towards the head. Keep it some centimeters over the head. As he trails the smell of the treat, his rear will drop to the ground while the front part will remain on the front legs.

The next technique is training the dog using a leash. Here, stand next to the dog while facing the same direction as the dog. Hold the leash straight and while saying "sit", push the dog's rump down, letting him sit down on the hind legs.

Down

You can start teaching this command by first getting the dog to sit down. Stand facing the dog while holding the dog treat on its nose and take it lower. Once the dog's belly is down and the front legs stretched out, give it the treat and then praise him.

If the dog fails to stretch out the front legs, move the treat horizontally and slowly away.

After the pet understands the non-verbal command, use the verbal command. Next time say the command as you lower the treat. The dog will be able to link the action with the command sooner.

Stay

Understanding the "down" and "sit" commands only don't show the dog's ability to understand commands. If the dog simply obeys a command and leaves once it's executed, you will lose the aim of teaching the commands.

Therefore, the dog should be taught to uphold the two initial commands till the release instruction is given. You can achieve this by training the dog to respect the "stay" command. Only teach this command once the dog has understood the previous two.

Stand facing the dog and then instruct it to either "down" or "sit." Keep eye contact and stay this way for one or two seconds. Praise the dog and offer him some treat and this will indicate the end of training time.

As he gets comfortable with shorter intervals of time, extend the time of upholding the "stay" position. After he reliably responds to this training level, add the verbal cue to your command.

Stand facing the dog and once he complies with the "down" or "sit" command, say "stay" while stretching out your hand with the palm facing him.

Come

This is the easiest command to teach, particularly for puppies. A puppy often sticks to the owner and enjoys playing around their feet. Getting him to his master isn't hard. Trying to get away from him may prove difficult.

Start with shorter distances. Step a couple of feet away from the puppy/dog. Hold a treat, kneel down and then call out the pet's name and command. For instance, "Tracy, come." With open arms, invite the dog to come.

As the dog starts to move in your direction, praise him. If he goes astray, quit praising and say the command again. If the dog starts walking towards you again, praise him. Reward the dog with praise and a treat once he reaches where you are.

Leave it

Teaching the dog the "leave it" command is valuable for several reasons. It keeps the dog safe. In case you drop medicine accidentally on the floor, he will leave it if told to. If there are broken glasses, simply utter "leave it." Use the command on anything you don't want the dog to interfere with.

The easiest way in teaching the "leave it" command is by using something that the dog wants, such as a toy or a treat. Choose something small that you can hold inside your palm.

While holding the treat with your fingers make sure that you let the dog to see, smell and even lick it. Then say the "leave it" command and move your hand away from him.

If he tries to follow your hand simply close your palm without letting him get to the treat. Only when he calms down or loses interest show him the treat, say the "leave it" command and again move your hand away. If he tries to grab it just close your palm with the treat inside.

Chapter 5:
House Manners For Dogs

When one has a dog in the house, particularly around the kids, they will want the dog to have some good house manners. This simply means that the dog is not hyperactive and will stay calm.

A dog with good house manners should not bother the kids while they are eating, or grab food off the table or counter. A dog that has house manners doesn't get into the garbage, eliminate on the floor or lay on the couch.

Rather, a good dog should be well behaved and be able to follow commands and rules. Here are some common house manners that dogs are expected to uphold as well as tips on how to teach them each manner.

House Essentials For Dogs

Staying within the designated area

Designate a place for the dog to stay in. This can be a crate, a dog bed, or a mat. Take your dog to the designated place and motivate him to stay right there. Give the dog treats and praise him.

Giving the dog a chew toy will aid in keeping it contented. It is advisable to get a crate for the dog since it will see it as a sanctuary. This will serve as a place to leave your dog in case you are going out of the house for some time.

Obeying the "leave it" command

After being quiet for about 10 minutes in the designated place, take him on a leash around the house. Point objects you may want him to just leave alone, and say "no" or "leave it."

The dog will obviously not understand this immediately and so you must redo this exercise repeatedly. If the dog insists on chewing things in your house, spray the objects with a bitter apple spray every 24 hours.

This is more effective when coupled with the "leave it" or "no" command.

Eliminating outside and not on the floor

Teach the dog to potty outside. When the dog is still learning manners, leash or put it in his crate. Be keen on the signals so that you take him outside before he actually relieves himself on the floor. While walking him around, praise him when he does well. They will figure out this very quickly and the secret is to be consistent.

Not bothering people when eating

Teach the dog not to beg, whine or jump up to get food from the table. You can achieve this by teaching him the "stay/down" command. Hold a treat, bring it close to the ground and then utter, "Down." In case he just bends the head to the treat, don't offer him the treat. Once he is down, give him the treat.

Teach him the "stay" command by gesturing stop with your hand as you say "stay." Slowly back away. If the dog attempts to follow, utter "no" and then walk him to his original position. Keep him in stay/down position a bit far from the table as you eat.

Not jumping on people

Teach the dog never to jump on strangers or you. When the dog jumps on you, utter "off", face away and ignore him completely until he is down. Once he's down, praise him well and show affection. The same should apply when the dog jumps on another person.

In conclusion, dogs are great pets. They are loyal and loving. With proper training, they will behave well in the house. Teach them like you will teach your kids, with patience and love.

Chapter 6:
F.A.Q. - Frequently Asked Questions

What is dog training?

The term dog training has several meanings. First, we have "behavior dog training" in which the dog is trained to be a "good citizen." This typically includes house training, reasonable leash manners, good behavior while they are around other dogs and people and other related things which make him a better companion.

We also have "obedience training," which generally teaches the dog how to do specific activities.

Finally, there is "activity training" which focuses on particular activities – like hunting, herding, lure coursing, search and rescue and other related activities that are used to showcase the capabilities of the dog.

How can I choose the right training?

There is no wrong or right training. There are training techniques that are more effective compared to others under some circumstances.

The things that one needs to take into consideration when they are choosing an effective method for their dogs include: their personality, the dog's personality, their goals and abilities as a trainer, and their experience as a trainer.

What is the difference between corrections and rewards?

Reward leads to an increase in a particular behavior while correction leads to the reduction in a particular behavior.

Rewards should be given such that they increase the behavior in question, meaning that it has to be something that motivates the dog and he enjoys too.

Why should I train my dog?

There are many numerous valid reasons why you should train a dog. It helps build the relationship between you and the dog, allows you to condition him to behave as you desire, and it enables you and the canine to live harmoniously.

Training is important in preventing undesired behaviors. Well trained dogs are often welcomed and liked in the entire society and neighborhood. Families who have well trained dogs are much happier because their dogs are always very eager to do some work for them.

According to experts, dog training is also healthy for dogs. In fact, many bad behavioral problems develop from lack of exercise.

Is it true that some dog breeds are "un-trainable?"

There is a perception that some dog breeds, such as the Beagles, are "un-trainable." But this is not the case, as all kinds of breeds from wolf hybrids to terriers to hounds can be trained well.

When is the right time to begin dog training?

Raising a pup is just like raising a baby. You should start training your puppy at an early stage, but it shouldn't be too early.

The right time to start training the puppy is from six to eight weeks. The puppy should learn habit-forming things at an early stage.

Which behavioral problems can dog training programs solve?

There are many behavioral problems that training can address. The common ones include jumping on people, destructive chewing, play biting, nuisance barking, getting on the furniture, and housebreaking.

Who is the boss when training the dog?

You must put some limits and rules so that the pet knows how it's required to behave. However, you don't have to instill good behaviors by force like pinning the pet on his side or pulling the choke chain.

Train your pets by rewarding their good behaviors as

soon as they successfully accomplish them and ensure that they are not rewarded for bad behavior.

Does positive reinforcement training means allowing your dog to do whatever he wants to?

Training the dog is like parenting. You should set limits and boundaries, and enforce them consistently.

This consistency would make it quite easier for the dog to master what you want. It would also reduce anxiety in the dog's life, as he knows what to do.

Conclusion

Training a dog requires time, patience and consistency. It can actually be both a simple and enjoyable process if you know how to properly train your dog in obedience. We hope this short guide provided you with useful information and helped you figure out the approach you should take with your own furry friend.

We will be more than happy to learn how this book has helped you in yours and your dog's life and the progress that you have made.

If you feel you have learned something or you think it offered you some value, please take a moment to leave an honest review on Amazon. It would help many future readers who will be forever grateful to you. As we will!

With Best Regards,
Vivaco Books

ALL RIGHTS RESERVED. No part of this publication may be reproduced or transmitted in any form whatsoever, electronic, or mechanical, including photocopying, recording, or by any informational storage or retrieval system without express written, dated and signed permission from the author.

DISCLAIMER AND/OR LEGAL NOTICES: Every effort has been made to accurately represent this book and it's potential. Results vary with every individual, and your results may or may not be different from those depicted. No promises, guarantees or warranties, whether stated or implied, have been made that you will produce any specific result from this book. Your efforts are individual and unique, and may vary from those shown. Your success depends on your efforts, background and motivation.

The material in this publication is provided for educational and informational purposes. Use of the programs, advice, and information contained in this book is at the sole choice and risk of the reader.

DOG OBEDIENCE TRAINING

The Definitive Guide To Effectively Train An Obedient Dog Without Being A Dog Whisperer

By Vivaco Books

Introdution

Contrary to popular belief, the art of dog training is not a reserve of professional dog trainers. With a little patience, a lot of passion, a flair for fun, and love for your pet, you can have your dog performing tricks and following your commands like a professional show dog.

Here is a fun fact. Did you know that dogs respond better to commands if they come from the trainer? It is a known fact that if you take your dog to a professional dog trainer chances are, the dog will respond to his or her command better than it would respond to your command once you take your dog or puppy home. How so?

Training gives the dog owner or in this case dog trainer, the opportunity to form a very strong bond with the pet. Any dog owner or lover should jump at the opportunity to train their dog, if not for the fun, for the fact that training affords you, the dog owner, a chance to influence your dog's behavior to suit your home settings.

With that said, let us learn about training our dogs.

Chapter 1: Dog Obedience Training 101: You Ought To Know This Before Training Your Dog

Other than the eternal bond that forms between you and your dog during training, there are other reasons why you should train your dog. If you have watched any popular dog film, I am sure the intelligence displayed by the dogs featured in the films did not fall short of spectacular. This could be your dog. You can train your dog to sit, fetch and other commands such as heel and lie down. Training will require gentleness and patience on your part. However, once you get the hang of it, there are no limits to the number of obedience commands you can train your dog to follow.

Getting started is as easy as snapping your finger. In fact, the most basic obedience training equipment you need is dog treats and a passion to teach your dog. In order to give you the motivation to train your dog, you may want to know the benefits of dog training.

Benefits Of Obedience Training (To Your Dog)

If you walk into the lobby of most hotels, you will notice a very strong message printed in bold, "no pets allowed." What do you think is the reason behind this?

Well, to be honest with you, the hotel managers are not at fault here. The people at fault are the dog owners who go to hotels with untrained dogs that leave a trail of havoc in the hotel hallways and rooms.

Imagine that, the reason there is a bold "no pets" sign, (some even go as far as to specify, "No untrained dogs allowed") is because a previous dog owner spoiled the chances of your dog being admitted there. Some hotels are very specific about the type of pets they allow into their perfect hotel rooms and an unruly, untrained dog falls in the category that is access restricted.

Access granted

A major motivator to undertake obedience training by any dog owner is the fact that well trained dogs and in extension, pets, are allowed into any hotel room because the managers of the said places (in this case, hotels) are sure that the owner has total command over their pet. After all, the hotel does not have a dedicated staff to run after unruly dogs. Training your dog to be obedient will allow your dog access to places that would have otherwise been restricted.

Additionally, if you train your dog to obey your commands, you can take him or her to a restaurant without causing a major kitchen or utensil catastrophe.

Sociable

I do not know whether you know this but most people would rather play or socialize with a trained dog. Dogs are very social creatures and social contact is a very important aspect of your dog's life. Training will not only increase your dog's chances of making friends, it will also improve the relationship between your trusted friend and other dogs.

The social part of training your dog will especially make it easier for your dog to interact with your family members and especially how to behave around your children. It is not unheard of for untrained dogs to cause physical harm to children.

A fundamental part of training is the fact that since the commands are very easy to master, even your children will be able to command your family dog when it starts to get excited and unruly which will happen a lot (dogs get excited easily).

Obedience training will allow you and your family to have more fun with the dog and offer you greater insight into the mind of your dog.

The learning curve

Fundamentally, training your dog is a good learning experience for the both of you. A fundamental fact to obedience training is that due to the easy nature of the commands, and the fact that you are using treats to entice and encourage your dog, it is fun and as we know, fun makes learning easier.

Obedience dog training like any normal human lesson, will give your dog a wealth of knowledge. The fun fact here is that regardless of your experience with dogs (whether you have had a dog for years or this is your first puppy) they are extremely easy to train. The only prerequisite to training is some enthusiasm.

You probably have heard this "you cannot teach an old dog new tricks"; this is not true (not entirely true anyway). It is not impossible to teach an old dog new tricks but it is easier to teach a puppy new tricks. The same methods that you would use to train a puppy are the same basic methods you would use to train an older dog with the only difference being the level of difficulty.

The learning curve goes both ways; your dog will learn, but so will you. If you decide to train your dog in the park, or enroll in a training program, you will interact with other dog owners who will enrich you with their fountain of knowledge (dog owners are usually very friendly to other dog owners).

Benefits Of Dog Training (To You)

A major reason and motivation to train your dog is the bond. The bond formed between you and your dog during training is unbreakable (even in old age).

However, other than the bond, here are few more reasons if you have not yet been convinced of training the dog yourself.

Better Control

Teaching your dog commands such as sit, stay, and other obedience commands will give you better control of your pet. This will automatically translate into better management. In essence, what this means is that once you train your dog, you can easily integrate him or her into any family activity rather than shutting him up in a crate.

Some obedience commands will allow you to call back your dog if he strays while you are walking him or, stop him from doing something that will embarrass you as a dog owner. While training my dog, I found that walking my dog got easier once we were through with training.

Additionally, training will make your pet ownership easier and fun. How so? Owning an untrained dog is sometimes complete chaos; the mess, poop everywhere, the howling at night. Once you train your dog, management becomes easier which in turn saves you lots of time and resources.

Safety

Earlier on, we had looked at the risks of leaving an untrained dog alone with your children. Training eliminates this risk and makes it safer for your young ones to be around the dog. An untrained dog or puppy is not only a risk to you and your family, but to himself.

This is not to say that a trained puppy will not hurt himself; it will (dogs will be dogs after all).

However, training will minimize this risk because once you notice the dog is getting over excited, you can command him or her to lie down. One instance that I have found training to be very effective is calling back the dog in dangerous scenarios like traffic.

Pride

I have had my dog for twelve years now. Something that never ceases to amaze me is the pride that builds up in my chest every time I am at the park and my dog obeys every command I give it. When I see someone struggling to control his or her dog, my pride skyrockets.

I am not only very proud of the bond and relationship between my beloved dog and me, but also very proud of the fact that over the years, with constant training, and the continued growth of our bond and relationship, my dog can anticipate my commands even before I offer them. This has turned me into a very proud owner.

Now that we have looked at some of the benefits of training your dog to obey your commands, let us look at some of the training devices available at your disposal.

Chapter 2: Obedience Training Devices - The Ones You Truly Need

The most critical tool you will need to train your dog is treats. However, some of the tools we shall discuss in this chapter will make the learning process easier. Nevertheless, there are those who believe that tools are less effective and sometimes crude, and thus hinder the development of the bond that forms between a dog and the owner in the manual training method.

It is almost impossible for me to come straight out and give you advice on the ideal tool to use on your dog, but the best advice I can offer here is to give you an overview of some of the most common devices used today.

Note: Whether you opt to use a training device or not, it is very important to note that on some dogs, using a training device (obedience or otherwise) may be counterproductive to the learning and training process. Therefore, it is very important to take note of your dog's behavior in order to notice which between the training device and the manual method of training is most effective.

More importantly, make sure that the device you opt to use is in no way harmful to your pet otherwise your dog will associate training with negative emotions.

Collars

A collar is a very popular dog-training device. Dog collars are the most important of all dog-training devices and they form the backbone of all other devices. There are five categories of dog collars, namely:

Flat collar
Slip collar
The Martingale collar
Prong collars
Shock collars

Each of these collars is effective on different types of dogs. To give you a better grasp of how each type works, it is only fair that we look at these five categories in details.

Flat collars

Flat collars are most effective in puppies. You will find flat collars in use at puppy kindergartens, mostly, to teach non-correction based training. Materials used to make the simplest flat collars are nylon and sometimes, leather fastened together with a quick release connection or buckle. This collar is very effective in training small dogs that other devices would fail to train.

As a disadvantage, using this collar on an overly excited or distracted dog will prove to be an enormous task. This is because the collar lifts the dog off the ground when correcting the dog's behavior, this is especially so when the dog is excited by new environments.

Slip collar

Choke or check-chains are the common names for the slip collar. This collar's main material is nylon and leather and sometimes, metal links. Today, slip collars are not as popular as they used to be. Traditionally, slip collars were common in the UK and North America to startle the dog to attention. By snapping and releasing the collar, you capture the dog's attention. A major reason why the use of this collar has declined is that if used improperly, it can lead to strangling.

Martingale collar

Martingale collars are also called limited slip collars; they are usually made of nylon with an additional short fixed length made from a short chain or nylon that when pulled, makes the collar around the dog's neck tighter. This type of collar is effective at correcting the behavior in an unruly dog.

Prong collars

A prong collar offers limited circumference around the dog's neck so that it is less constrictive. Part of the reason for the change in design in the prong collar is so that the collar does not pinch or hurt the dog when pulled.

Note: If you fasten a prong collar improperly, you risk the chance of causing bodily harm to your dog. The safest way to use this collar is by placing plastic tips on the split ends of prongs to stop the formation of clumps in the fur.

Shock collars

Shock collars are electronic collars capable of receiving a signal from a device controlled by the dog owner. The shock collar also E-collar, works by transmitting a controlled electric current that jolts a barking dog and stops the barking.

The shock collar is also very effective in ensuring that a dog wearing the collar stays in its boundary. Of all the collars we have looked at, the shock collar is the most conventional. Some dog trainers, vet professionals and kennel club members swear by its effectiveness.

A collar is a very effective tool when teaching your dog most of the obedience commands we shall look at later. Other than the collars, you will come across some other devices in your dog training endeavors, some of which will include:

Leash

A leash is very popular and perhaps one of the most popular dog training and handling devices. It connects the dog to the owner in order to lead the dog in the intended direction especially in urban settings, which have laws against unrestrained dogs. The type of leash material you opt to buy will largely depend on your preferences as a dog owner, because leashes come from different materials such as nylon, metal, or leather.

Today, it is almost impossible to walk a dog without using a leash. A leash will form a very crucial part of your dog training and I would suggest you take some time to find and select the proper leash for your dog.

Clicker

Unlike humans, dogs can hear sounds on a different frequency. A clicker, a small hand device, is one of these devices that make a sound in the frequency that only dogs can hear.

You can use a clicker to signal your dog to follow a command associated with the sound. While training my dog, I found that the clicker was especially effective in calling back my puppy if he strayed too far while we were in the park.

Over the years, the clicker has gained popularity as an ideal training tool. This is because you can train your dog without the need for physical correction. Perhaps I should also mention that this tool is not very effective on its own, and will work best if followed by other methods of training.

Head Halter

Dog head halters are an adaptation of the horse halter. They are a good alternative to the collars we looked at earlier. A head halter fits over the snout and head of the dog, which in effect, makes it easier to control and lead the dog. The halter makes it impossible for the dog to pull on the leash.

However, this does not necessarily mean that the dog is completely incapable of pulling on the leash. Remember this when using a head halter; do not apply a lot of pressure on the halter otherwise, the dog will suffer injuries on the neck.

Chapter 3: 6 Mistakes Beginners Usually Make and How to Avoid Them

In the beginning, it is almost inevitable and somewhat acceptable to make mistakes. However, it is very critical to restrict your mistake to occasional slip-ups otherwise you will end up with a trained dog that is unable to follow when you utter a command.

The six mistakes we shall look at are very common and many dog owners and trainers are guilty of committing them. It is my hope that by understanding these mistakes, you shall avoid them and make the learning process easier for both you and your dog.

#Mistake No1: Wrong thing right time/ Right thing wrong time

Being affectionate to your dog while he is being unruly or a nuisance will send the wrong message. For instance, if you pet your puppy while he is barking, you are sending the message that barking is ok. What this does is that it makes the dog associate the barking with the petting.

Solution: Remember that your dog associates petting and treats with the activity it was doing. More importantly, only show affection or offer a treat to your dog only when he or she is performing the desired action.

#Mistake No2: The gentle but firm giant

When you begin the training, you will be tempted to cut your dog some slack. This is especially when you are taking him or her for a walk on a leash. Do not get me wrong, it is okay to let the dog lead you, but more importantly, the dog needs to know their boundaries.

You need to be firm and gentle when pulling them back on the leash. In the initial stages of training, your dog will yank the leash and sprint ahead of you. This can be very dangerous and not to mention tiresome.

Solution: Set boundaries. Let your dog know that to in order to get food, they have to stop being excited, sit, and wait patiently. When you are walking him, entice him to walk close to your side by offering treats and praises when he does so and gently castigating him when he yanks on the leash (bad boy/ girl seems to work well). Using a firm voice is also very effective in showing your pet who is the master.

Point to note: Do not be tempted to use overly verbose language or your pup will think you are angry with him. Find a balance between firm and gentle.

#Mistake No3: Lest you forget

Another mistake you are bound to make in the initial stages of training is to think that your dog has the same comprehension and understanding as a human. You have to understand that even though training your dog will be easy, dogs have a way of thinking that is completely different from humans. Science would say that you and your dog are different species; you are a homo sapiens and your dog is a Canis lupus.

This '"mistaking your dog for a human" is especially common in new dog owners who tend to think that a dog will conceptualize a command the same way a human would. You will be tempted to slap your dog when you utter a command and he just wags his tail. You may be tempted to yell the command repeatedly but I assure you this will not work. Exercise patience (restraint will also help).

Solution: Even though your dog will be an integral part of your family, remember that he is not like you. Treat your dog as you would treat a child who is discovering the world; remember that a dog experiences the world in a different unique way.

#Mistake No4: Hygiene is not a compromise

Occasionally your dog will bite or scratch you. When this happens, you risk infection if the hygiene of your dog is not up to par. Most dog owners forget to clip the nails on their dog's paws, brush their teeth, wash, and dry their fur. If you cannot brush your dog's teeth on a daily basis, try to do it several times a week or your dog will develop gum disease.

In this same breath, most young mutts are very playful and yours will play in the dirt all day long. Failing to clean your dog can lead to a lice infestation or worse.

Cleaning (hygiene in general) will preempt some of the more serious problems that are because of a tiny problem such as gum disease.

Solution: To avoid the mess of dirt all over your home, I suggest you build a playpen with some sea sand. To reduce your vet bill (when you let the bad breath develop into something more), groom your dog's paws and teeth. If grooming is a problem (for whatever reason), you can always schedule a grooming session for your pup.

#Mistake No5: Show some love to the crate

If you are one of those dog owners who loath the crate, you are missing out. Dogs are by nature den animals and a crate is as close as it gets to a den. Dogs are always looking out for "safe" places to call their own, and in this case, the crate is just that.

By crate training, you get more flexibility even when

travelling, and your dog gets a space he can associate with his wild side.

Solution: Make sure that while crate training your dog, you do not traumatize the dog otherwise, he will associate the crate with negative emotions. Remember that crate training is an advanced skill that you should not try until you have created a bond with your dog and taught him or her some obedience training.

#Mistake No6: Looking at training from a negative side

We have looked at this; approaching training with a negative mentality will leave your dog with a very unsavory experience. True to this, a number of studies have shown that using positive reinforcement is 57% more effective than using punishment and dominance.

Additionally, the same studies have shown that using dominance and punishment training will cause your dog to develop other undesirable behaviors and make the training process harder.

Solution: Give your dog a treat when he is responsive to a command and be firm in a gentle way when castigating him. Positive reinforcement is the best way to achieve result rapidly.

We have now looked at everything you need to know, have, and be aware of before moving into the actual obedience training. Before proceeding to the next chapter, please take some time to review everything we have learnt so far. Once you are done with this, head to the next chapter equipped with enthusiasm, patience and all devices and treats you intend to use.

Chapter 4: Basic Training: How To Properly Teach Your Dog These 5 Essential Commands

This is the most exciting chapter in this book. In this chapter, we are moving from the theory part of learning into the practical training. To get us started, we shall begin with some of the most fundamental obedience commands and progressively build up to the advanced commands.

How to teach your dog the sit command

As far as dog obedience commands go, it does not get any easier than the sit command. This command will go a long way into making your dog more controllable. Once your dog has mastered this command, he will not get overly excited when the doorbell rings and thus, will be more controllable when your visitors walk in.

To begin this process:

#1 Put your dog's favorite treat in your hand and drop to the same level as your dog. Ideally, you should drop to the floor.

#2 With the treat enclosed in your palm, bring it close to the dog's muzzle and make sure that he or she sniffs the treat. When you are sure that the dog has recognized the smell, slowly raise your treat hand.

Note: Do not raise the arm too high as this might cause your dog to jump up to reach for it.

#3 If the dog does not respond, repeat one and two above. Make sure that your hand is in an inclination that forces the dog to sit. Once you notice that he or she has gone into the sit position reward him with the treat, some encouragement, and some affection. Make sure to repeat this process a few times daily to associate this behavior with the sit command.

How to teach your dog the down command

The down command is very effective, especially when dealing with an unruly dog. Unlike other simple commands, the down command is a bit difficult for dogs to learn because it is a submissive command which dogs are not very comfortable with.

A fundamental truth to teaching this command is

that you need a lot of positive reinforcement.

To get started:

#1 Use either of your hands to enclose a treat and bring the treat close to the dog's muzzle ensuring that the dog gets a whiff of the treat.

#2 When sure that the dog has noticed the scent of the treat enclosed in your palm, move the hand down in the direction of the floor and ensure that the dog follows this movement.

#3 Once the dog starts following the "treat enclosed hand", move the hand across the floor towards him. The dog will stretch out in a down position. Offer him the treat once he is in this position and praise him or her.

#4 As in the earlier command, perform this a few times a day to associate this process with the down command. More importantly, when your dog lunges for the treat (which he or she will), remember to be a firm but gentle giant and use a firm "no" while moving your hand away from your dog.

Note: While practicing this command, you will be tempted to force your dog into the down position. Restrict yourself; this is counterproductive to the learning process.

How to teach your dog the heel command

The heel command is not your typical obedience command. In fact, most dog trainers and vets refer to it as an advanced dog training command. Nevertheless, in my personal opinion, it is by far more useful than other commands and therefore I have included it in the basic section of this book.

To teach the command:

#1 Move to a familiar environment (preferably at home), and place the dog at your side (not touching you).

#2 Hold a treat in your enclosed palm, and place the hand close to your waist. Now call out to your dog. (this will work better if you are facing the dog and maintaining eye contact).

#3 When you capture the dog's attention, take two steps forward, and stop. If your dog follows, while still in the heel position, offer him the treat and praise him.

#4 When he is done with the treat, repeat the above process immediately and praise him when he accomplishes the task successfully. Once he can follow the command successfully, attach a verbal command to the physical process.

How to teach your dog the come command

The come command will come in handy when you are dealing with an unruly dog or puppy. It is a very easy command to teach and will require a collar or leash.

Let us get started:
#1 Clip a collar and light line onto your dog and let

him or her drag this around for a few hours.

#2 After a few hours, grab the end of the line and walk around with your dog (the dog will recognize this as an attachment between the two of you). Do not forget to carry a few treats.

#3 After aimlessly walking around with your dog (letting him drag you) move in the opposite direction and encourage your dog to follow by beckoning him. When he starts following, encourage him with positive words such as yes or good boy/girl and offer him or her a treat.

#4 Repeat the procedures above a few times during the day and when the dog is acquainted with the command, couple it with the verbal "come" command.

How to teach your dog the stay command

This command is the most effective of all commands especially in controlling a very unruly dog.

To begin:

#1 Place the dog on a leash and sit next to him or on the same level. Use your palm to gain the dog's attention by waving it close to his muzzle and asking him to stay in a gentle but commanding voice.

#2 Step in front of your dog and hold your pose for a little while. If the dog stays, move back to your former position besides him and offer him a treat and some well-deserved praise.

#3 Like every obedience command we have practiced so far, repeat this one a few times in a day and if the dog breaks the command, firmly tell him "no" or "Uh Uh". After your dog has obeyed the above command several times, associate the process with the verbal "stay" command.

Note: While teaching the above obedience commands, do not move at a very fast pace, remember that dogs have a lower span of concentration (especially for older dogs).

Chapter 5: Advanced Training: Three Advanced Commands For Dogs - Are You Ready To Kick It Up A Notch?

After your dog has learnt the basic obedience commands, you might want to kick it up a notch higher. In this chapter, we shall look at 3 common advanced dog-training commands that you can teach your dog.

How to teach your dog the "watch me" command

As I have said numerously throughout this book, dogs have a very short attention span. Therefore, it is important to teach your dog the watch me command that is geared towards increasing your dog's attention.

To train your dog:
#1 Enclose a treat in your hand and sit in in front of your dog.

#2 Your dog's nose is very sensitive and he will smell the treat. When you notice the dog turning his or her head, calmly but authoritative utter the "watch me" command and give him the treat if he follows the command.

Note: Avoid staring at your dog for more than a few seconds at a time because the dog will translate this as a challenge.

How to teach your dog the "place" command

The place command is good for moving your dog to a designated place such as the crate.

To teach this command:

#1 Choose a place you want to associate with this command (this can be any word and any location such as bed, crate etc.). Put your dog on a leash and lead him to the location you have chosen. Once in this place, use the affirmative "yes" to indicate the association and offer the dog a treat and some encouragement.

#2 Without removing the leash, repeat this command a couple of times until you are certain the dog has understood the command. When sure, remove the leash and give the command. If the dog responds, offer him a treat and some encouragement. After your dog has obeyed the above command several times, associate the process with the verbal "place" command.

How to teach your dog the "steady" command

The steady command will be your go to command when fighting to control an unruly dog. To teach it, you will need a four inch raised platform, an E-collar and a crate.

#1 The raised platform can be a piece of plywood that will act as the dog's place board and as an identifying "stay" place until you release him.

#2 Place a crate 12 inches from the raised board. Ensure that the crate door is open.

#3 Let the dog become familiar with the crate; when he enters, leave him there and utter the stay command and move away from the crate (ensure the crate door is open so that the dog can leave when he desires).

#4 When the dog steps off the board, press the button on the transmitter and utter the "steady" command.

#5 Let the dog relax for a while and when you see that he is hesitant to step off the board, it means that he has comprehended that to keep the collar of; he has to stay on the board.

Conclusion

Teaching your dog all the above commands is not as hard as you thought, right? I am sure by now you and your dog have had a lot of fun time learning and teaching the basic and advanced commands we have looked at.

As a last piece of advice, learning for a dog never stops, so continue teaching your dog new tricks every day. Experiment with many commands and you and your dog will be better off.

If you feel you have learned something or you think it offered you some value, please take a moment to leave an honest review on Amazon. It would help many future readers who will be forever grateful to you. As we will!

With Best Regards,
Vivaco Books

ALL RIGHTS RESERVED. No part of this publication may be reproduced or transmitted in any form whatsoever, electronic, or mechanical, including photocopying, recording, or by any informational storage or retrieval system without express written, dated and signed permission from the author.

DISCLAIMER AND/OR LEGAL NOTICES: Every effort has been made to accurately represent this book and it's potential. Results vary with every individual, and your results may or may not be different from those depicted. No promises, guarantees or warranties, whether stated or implied, have been made that you will produce any specific result from this book. Your efforts are individual and unique, and may vary from those shown. Your success depends on your efforts, background and motivation.

The material in this publication is provided for educational and informational purposes. Use of the programs, advice, and information contained in this book is at the sole choice and risk of the reader.

Printed in Great Britain
by Amazon